vid Mach **Temple at Tyre**

ook represents a permanent record of a dramatic
– the construction of *Temple at Tyre* on Leith Docks
vember 1994.

mple at Tyre, commissioned by Edinburgh District
il, was the largest piece of temporary public art ever
n the UK. It was designed and constructed by David
, the internationally-renowned Scottish sculptor.

vork built on Edinburgh's reputation for staging
art events of international significance, such as *Lux*
æ during the 1992 European Summit.

e other challenging art works, the massive sculpture
ted admirers and detractors in equal measure – for
onth it was on view, it was impossible to ignore.
e from viewpoints throughout Edinburgh, and even
the air, *Temple at Tyre* reinforced the city's dramatic
e and reflected local landmarks like Calton Hill with
ssical temple, started in the 1820s but never finished.

mple at Tyre signals Edinburgh's commitment to
public places through the Percent for Art scheme,
he importance of the Leith waterfront as a key site
generation and redevelopment in the lead-up to the
2000.

mple at Tyre could not have been built without
enerous sponsorship of Kwik-Fit, Wimpey Homes
Forth Ports PLC, and the support of many other
companies and individuals.

FORTH PORTS PLC

BK14592

David Mach

Temple at Tyre

Temple at Tyre Richard Cork

As winter advanced on Edinburgh in the closing months of 1994, the bleakness of the old dockland area at Leith was alleviated. With surprising speed, a colossus arose on the water's edge. A desolate stretch of flattened land at Victoria Dock was suddenly transformed into the site for the largest temporary public art-work ever erected in Britain. Size alone, of course, could not ensure that the sculpture was worth looking at. Grand monuments are often unforgiveably dull or pompous, and their vastness offers no guarantee that anyone will notice them. But David Mach's *Temple at Tyre* seized attention at once, and will not easily be forgotten by anyone who encountered its hallucinatory presence.

The sense of strangeness depended, above all, on the fusion of disparate images. The 145 shipping containers assembled on the waterfront did not look out of place there. Mach stacked them in a matter-of-fact fashion, eschewing rhetorical gestures in favour of a sober, minimalist approach. These steel boxes might have been waiting to serve some functional role, but the structure surmounting them belonged to a wholly different world. Nobody would expect to find a full-blown classical temple in such a context. It looked at first glance like a transplanted Parthenon, momentarily resting

en route between Athens and some alien northern destination far removed from the consoling warmth of the Aegean.

Closer inspection revealed, however, that this building had not been carved from a Greek quarry. On the contrary: pillars, pediment and roof alike were made of 8,000 tyres. The sculpture's title, therefore, has a double meaning. As well as referring to the ancient seaport of Tyre, that once-formidable Phoenician centre for Mediterranean trade, it draws attention to the far less romantic fact that used tyres from a Kwik-Fit dump supplied the raw materials for the temple. Moreover, Mach made no attempt to hide their identity. Just as he accepted and exposed the rawness of the containers, so he disclosed exactly how the tyres had been placed on top of each other in the completed building.

In this respect, he still adheres to a 'truth to materials' philosophy acquired during his sculptural training at the Duncan of Jordanstone College of Art in Dundee. Mach abhors the whole notion of disguising the often unconventional elements he uses, and their open proclamation forms a vital part of his work's meaning.

He first deployed tyres in 1983, when invited to

make a large outdoor sculpture for a show staged in and around the Hayward Gallery. The exhibition's principal sponsor was the United Technologies Corporation, responsible for the production of nuclear weapons. So Mach's decision to build a half-size version of a Polaris submarine, with 6,000 tyres, inevitably carried a polemical sting. In the event, the sculpture was vandalised by an arsonist who accidentally killed himself in the process. So the submarine became the most celebrated of Mach's early works. But before it was burned, the sculpture's commanding impact resided in a brazen reliance on a material laughably divorced from the sleek, aggressive products of the nuclear defence industry.

Compared with a Polaris, the tyres seemed defiantly old-fashioned and almost innocent. When applied to a temple, though, they take on a very different character. Pitched against its venerable associations, the rubber discs appear heretical in their modernity. A temple, after all, should be a place of worship. The only deity invoked by the use of tyres is the motor-car, and the fact that no one can enter Mach's edifice, rules out religious services altogether. Even if anyone was intrepid or foolhardy enough to climb up to the temple's facade, the entrance is sealed. Where its interior and spiritual heartland should be, containers block the way. This is an uncompromisingly secular building, using the trappings of classicism simply as a means of dignifying a mercantile core.

By robbing his temple of its traditional role, Mach invites us to think about how the language of classical architecture is deployed elsewhere in Edinburgh. Although the city has long enjoyed the flattering soubriquet 'the Athens of the North', the truth is that many of its most redoubtable frontages dress up businesses driven by tough, unashamedly commercial ambitions. Banks, insurance companies and building societies all bask in their classical trappings, which lend them an air of reliability. They look solid enough to inspire confidence, and appear to have been standing there for eternity. Bent on generating awe, they seem unshakeably rooted in the bedrock of Scotland.

The reality, however, is far less immutable. Edinburgh, like most other major western cities, has only acquired these noble facades over the past three centuries. The businesses housed inside them have experienced plenty of vicissitudes, and their apparent determination to remain firmly in one place, masks manifold and accelerating links with multinational interests. Money travels faster than ever as the millenium's end approaches. The bank's portico may still be attached to a particular plot of land, but the activities within make geographical boundaries dissolve at will.

In its own quirky and unexpected way, Mach's temple gives this paradox outward expression. The classical facade is restated, in an immediately recognisable form, and yet the tyres point towards a dynamism at odds with stately somnolence. After all, they are associated with vehicles moving at speed. Tyres mean mobility, not putting down roots. They are meant to drive forward rather than stand still on an eminence as imposing as the Acropolis or, to take the most self-consciously Athenian example in Edinburgh, Calton Hill. Unlike the latter, where Sir William Playfair's unfinished National Monument strives to disguise its 19th-century origins and look immemorial, the temple at Leith seemed restless. Although the tyres were stacked in a very precise and rigorous way, they appeared ready at any second to be disassembled and returned to their proper context.

So did the containers beneath. While contributing

The outcome lacked the soaring grandeur of the Leith version, and the stacking of the tyres around a wooden skeleton means that the pillars at Middelheim look more unstable than their taut counterparts in the Edinburgh sculpture. All the same, the Antwerp temple has an aura of longevity. It appears to be part of the richly foliated parkland setting, where visitors encounter the sculpture as they might come across an ancient, abandoned building in the middle of an overgrown forest.

No such romantic connotations could have been aroused by the school playground where Mach made another temple in 1993. This time, the sculpture was installed in the uncompromisingly urban setting of the Byker estate in Newcastle. So the temple rested on tarmac rather than grass, and looked frankly bizarre surrounded by school buildings and public housing which could only have been designed in the latter half of the present century.

Once again, the result appeared more securely lodged and earthbound than *Temple at Tyre* would become. But Mach, who has always enjoyed collaborating with assistants on large sculptural projects, was enormously stimulated by the half-dozen Geordies who helped him build the Byker work. Their enthusiasm for rock-climbing and, more specifically, abseiling, prompted Mach to start thinking about a far taller base for his temple. The stories they told him about the exhilaration of descending a precipitous hillside made him realise that *Temple at Tyre* would gain enormously from elevation. And since containers already provided the structural core of the Byker sculpture, the most straightforward solution involved extending them downwards until they formed an appropriately monumental base.

By doing so, Mach ensured that the containers

in large part to the towering impact of the sculpture, they provided no affirmation of permanence. Despite their formidable bulk and collective height, these ribbed units lacked finality. They seemed ready for action, merely pausing before the next frenetic bout of packing and travelling.

Their temporality becomes even more overt when compared with Mach's previous attempts to make a restatement of the Parthenon in the late 20th century. The first of his temples arose at the Middelheim Museum in Antwerp, where he was invited to work in the summer of 1985. With the help of 6,000 tyres, he built his structure on a modest base raised only slightly above the grass.

took on a powerful identity of their own. They came out of hiding, and at night flamboyant floodlighting ensured that their colours played a decisive role in giving the sculpture a surprising amount of resplendence. It burned on the side of Victoria Dock, and cast an equally inflamed reflection in the water. Seen *in toto*, the temple and its shimmering inverted image resembled a fantastical mirage.

For all the sturdiness of its construction, *Temple at Tyre* vanished almost as quickly as a dream. Commissioned by a city council eager to promote Edinburgh's vitality as a centre of architectural excellence, it was dismantled before the year's end. In one sense, the sculpture's fleeting lifespan deprived the city of a landmark worth preserving. But its ephemerality seems appropriate as well. The disappearance of Mach's *tour de force* accords with his emphasis on the principle of perpetual movement. Besides, it was memorable enough to become permanent in the minds of many who admired it. Rather than lingering there so long that everyone began to take it for granted, the sculpture departed while still a fresh and provocative presence.

How can its legacy be summarised? By focusing on the central paradox of a monument constructed from materials associated with driving and shipping, Mach implied that Edinburgh, and any other European capital, should never lapse into a complacent reiteration of historical precedents. Even the greatest city will ossify if it fails to understand the continual need for bold, imaginative renewal. Conservation alone is insufficient, and the inhabitants of the nearby Scottish Office would do well to ponder this lesson as they gaze out at the land where *Temple at Tyre* once blazed out its challenge, warning us not to rely exclusively on the beguiling, often deceptive achievements of the past.

Building Temple at Tyre David Mach

In 1986, I wrote about wanting to create a 'sculpture hit squad'. A team which would travel to a venue, work to a deadline to put a sculpture together, jump into the back of a van, drive to the airport, fly to the next venue and make a sculpture there and so on. The squad never became a regular group of people but since 1986 I have worked with many different members in venues all over the world. Temple at Tyre is the squad's latest achievement.

To make a sculpture in this way is to make a performance, to perform live. Temple at Tyre, not a shy, retiring piece, does not exist within the protective environs of a museum. It demands its audience, it demands to be seen. It's the kind of project I love, it's big and dramatic, physically as well as mentally demanding, done against the clock. Making it with my hit squad of Geordies, makes it all the more vital, all the more contentious, all the more live.

The same Geordies built the previous temple on the Byker Estate in Newcastle in 1993. That temple was a replica of the original one I made in Antwerp in 1985. It wasn't something I wanted to repeat again, once was enough. The 'Byker Boys' showed me how to develop this idea into the Temple at Tyre. They are all abseilers and through talking to them about abseiling, it became clear to me that the way to develop my sculpture was through its foundations. It followed logically that as the temple was already built around eight 20' freight containers, it would be a simple matter to extend them down until they became the hill or mountain that the temple sits on, and which we would have to climb up and could abseil down.

At Leith we did have to climb up the containers to build, but we never did get around to abseiling down it, although it was still a very raunchy show. As a team we had to 'lay' tyres, we had to 'erect' scaffolding and containers and we were very sexily buckled and strapped into our safety gear.

In fact, the performance and paraphenalia of this piece were so high, that it is difficult for me to separate the performance from the sculpture's meaning or at least what I want it to mean. Not that this is necessarily desirable when you are actually working / performing. My tendency then is to follow my instincts, but it is one of the pitfalls of working in public spaces with contemporary art, that the artist is asked 'What is it all about?'

No one would even think about asking a singer what his / her music is about while they are actually singing. Nor would anyone ask a wrestler what it

had thought that I was making maquettes for bigger pieces – to aid their making – but I revise that now. These smaller temples, some still big enough to be made with car tyres, others with toy car tyres, are sculptures in their own right. They will stand on their own or appear together at different locations, all made on different foundations.

The temple make of car tyres already challenges the notion of permanence and respectability. A tyre might be seen as a nomadic thing, something always on the move, never standing still. A temple, Greek or otherwise, seems to have become an abused image. It is immediately associated with stability and permanence, reliability, something to trust. That's why banks, insurance companies, religions, et cetera, adopt this image so readily. I question 'trusting' like that.

Changing the foundations challenges that trust even further and they are a vital element in the

feels like to have someone's elbow trying to gouge out your eye while he is actually rolling around the canvas. Admittedly this is a bit of a self-inflicted injury for artists as we are such windbags, but the truth is also that most artists don't know exactly what is going on since they are also involved in experimentation.

Finishing *Temple at Tyre* in Leith, however, has cleared up some confusion for me and turned one temple into a long series of continually developing ideas.

Immediately, *Temple at Tyre* has become the biggest in a series of eight or nine temples. Like a set of babushka dolls, the first temple small enough to hold in the palm of your hand, the last, *Temple at Tyre,* big enough to climb up and abseil down. I

development of these sculptures. In Leith, 145 containers were welded and locked together providing a solid and substantial base. And yet a couple of weeks after dismantling, they could be scattered to the four winds and end up in 145 different locations.

These are important objects, to me a container is one of the most significant objects of our time.

They are truly international: an Eskimo knows what a container is, so does an Aborigine. They are at once a fantastic building block, they are a minimal Greek Temple in themselves, with their classically ribbed sides. They have 'contained' almost everything we buy these days, all of our worldly goods have been transported in these boxes and when

11

they are sealed and used as mini bonded warehouses they even control the price of some of those goods. (Fill a container with cigarettes at pre-Budget prices and afterwards make a tidy profit.) They are a logical extension from the artist's boxes of Schwitters and Cornell.

Sit down and watch the telly and containers crop up quite a lot – watch a tank being loaded into one for transport to the nearest war, see people living in a city made of them in earthquake-struck Georgia.

In short, they shape our world significantly and quite literally 'contain' it. To 'contain' in this sense means to 'limit'. I don't want to be limited, I don't want to be held back, stopped from developing, pigeonholed, taped or boxed in, and I don't want anyone else to be either. And so *Temple at Tyre* doesn't finish at Leith. It will appear again, atop other objects. If I can, I will build a floating version on top of a super tanker and see it move on the back of ten articulated lorries across a football field.

Art in Public Spaces in Scotland Robert Breen

David Mach's *Temple at Tyre* is undoubtedly the artist's largest and most ambitious temporary public art work to date, but it is not his first in Edinburgh. In 1985, the city commissioned Art in Partnership to curate a temporary exhibition for its first Spring Festival and we invited a number of national and international artists to make new works or locate existing sculptures in Princes Street Gardens. Scottish artists David Mach and Doug Cocker and Bernard Pagès from France were among several artists invited to design and make new works in the Gardens. Their sculptures, which were made on site, gave the public a rare opportunity to observe the normally private process of making a work of art.

When artists move outside the studio into the public realm, the practice of making art becomes less a single individual activity – as in the case of painting – and more an opportunity for collaboration and the exchange of ideas. The Princes Street Gardens project and other temporary projects, where artists have been given the opportunity to make work outside the gallery context, have helped to generate debate and widen the interest in public art in Scotland.

Temporary public art projects give artists the

Edinburgh Spring Fling 1989: sculptures in Princes Street Gardens by David Mach *(top)* and Bernard Pagès *(bottom)*

opportunity and the freedom to explore new ideas and issues, sometimes on a scale that would be difficult or even impossible in a museum or gallery context. It can have a greater impact than its permanent counterpart: art works seen on a daily basis can become too familiar, even invisible, whereas a successful temporary work such as George Wyllie's *Straw Locomotive* (a full-sized straw train suspended from the Finnieston crane in Glasgow) which was finally set alight, or David Mach's *Temple at Tyre*, remain etched in our memories and influence our ideas over a long period of time.

To date, these opportunities have been comparatively rare in Scotland, although events such as the 1988 Glasgow Garden Festival and the *Lux Europae* event in Edinburgh in 1992 gave artists from Scotland and abroad scope to experiment and to collaborate with professionals from other disciplines, including engineers, landscape designers and architects. Equally important, these events introduced the concept of art in public places to a new public.

Temporary and permanent public art will always

Patricia Leighton *Sawtooth Ramps* 1993, M8 Art Project, Livingston, West Lothian

be interdependent. The best permanent public art projects stimulate questions about the past and the present of our built environment. The most effective temporary public art projects can help us find the way forward. Several of the most innovative public art projects in Scotland incorporate both of these elements.

The M8 Art Project, launched in 1993, has plans for a six-year programme of temporary, community-orientated projects, to run alongside a series of major permanent commissions throughout the Edinburgh to Glasgow road corridor.

The first of these is a major land work piece – *Sawtooth Ramps* by Patricia Leighton, a Scottish artist now based in New York. The commissioner, Motorola, selected the artist from an international competition, and the work was completed in 1993. Her proposal referred to the West Lothian landscape and made intelligent use of local resources, perfectly reflecting the company's environmental policy and its desire to reach the local community. The project has also given the motorway public, which makes 36 million journeys each year across Scotland's busiest trunk road, a unique and much-needed landmark.

By 1996, three major projects are expected to be in place. Louise Scullion and Matthew Dalziel's magical proposal for Polkemmet Country Park in West Lothian and David Mach's brilliantly apposite proposal for a massive steel sculpture to mark the new Mossend terminal, will rely on securing a complex mix of public and private funding.

This initial stage of the M8 Art Project has achieved significant support among a wide range of interests – from central and local government authorities to the police, environmentalists, road-user groups and business – for the concept of a series of artworks along the M8. The project is also

14

attracting international attention with enquiries from transport authorities as far away as Australia and Japan.

Innovative public art projects in Scotland are not confined to the Central Belt: 1994 saw the inauguration of the Tyrebagger Sculpture Project, a new public art led arts-tourism project in the North-East.

The concept of artists and crafts people being invited to undertake residencies in working forests is already well established in the UK. Projects in Grizedale Forest, Cumbria and the Forest of Dean in Gloucestershire have been extremely successful in attracting a remarkable number of visitors each year. Grizedale in particular, has established a reputation which now extends well beyond Cumbria and the UK.

For the Tyrebagger Sculpture project to succeed in Kirkhill Forest near Aberdeen it must not only provide an attractive amenity for the local community, it must also aim to become a cultural destination for visitors to the North-East of Scotland. It will not be enough to repeat the Grizedale formula, as this would ignore the many positive factors that make the Tyrebagger project unique. Unlike Grizedale, the location of Kirkhill Forest, close to the city of Aberdeen, means the project can benefit from the wide range of skills and resources that the city has to offer.

David Mach's proposal to work with an Aberdeen storyteller and author on a project for Tyrebagger would seem to have little in common with *Temple at Tyre*. But the sponsors of both events are well aware that properly considered public art projects can make an invaluable contribution to the success of a coherent arts-tourism strategy.

Edinburgh's bid for the 1999 Year of Architecture and Design and David Mach's project at Victoria Quay also provided an opportunity for the city to

Allan Watson *Beacon* 1994, Tyrebagger Sculpture Project, Kirkhill Forest, Aberdeenshire

reaffirm its commitment to public art. Edinburgh was among the first local authorities in Scotland to endorse a Percent for Art policy and support the principle of involving artists and craftspeople in its plans for the future of its historic centre and expanding peripheral developments.

But like many other authorities, it has been slow to put policy into practice. If events such as the bid for the Year of Architecture and Design 1999 and the *Temple at Tyre* project have been successful in generating a more informed public debate in Scotland, then it may open the way for new partnerships between artists and the increasingly large teams of specialists and officials responsible for redefining and reshaping our public spaces in Scotland.

Temple at Tyre was made possible
by generous sponsorship from Kwik-Fit,
Wimpey Homes and Forth Ports PLC.

The project was managed by Scotland's
leading public art commissions agency,
Art in Partnership.

Edinburgh District Council would also like to thank
the following for their support and assistance:

ADN ENGINEERING

AINSCOUGH CRANE HIRE

ARCHITECTURAL LIGHTING DESIGN COMPANY

DAVID NARRO ASSOCIATES

JOHN McMENAMIN BUILDING CONTRACTORS

O'ROURKE & SONS

PAR SCAFFOLDING

THE RUSSELL GROUP

Thanks to the 'hit squad': Dave, Tony, Sean,
Steve and Kevin. A significant part of that squad
acts behind the scenes. Art in Partnership played
an essential role in the completion of the sculpture
– thanks to Rob, Sam and Lesley – if they hadn't
moved with such speed it would never have
happened. Thanks also to Tom Kennedy and
Giselle Dye and everyone else at the Bid Office, to
George Kerevan for suggesting it to Edinburgh in
the first place, and thanks to Edinburgh District
Council for commissioning the sculpture. Lastly,
and most importantly, thanks to Kwik-Fit and
Wimpey Homes for their very valuable sponsorship, and to Forth Ports, and all the other
companies and individuals who gave their time
and help so generously.

David Mach

Published by
The City of Edinburgh District Council
City Chambers, High Street,
Edinburgh EH1 1YJ
© Edinburgh District Council 1995

ISBN 0 9525219 0 3

Photography by Lloyd Smith
Additional photography by
Ant Critchfield (pages 7, 23 & 24)
Robin Gillanders (page 34)
David Williams (page 33)
Designed and typeset by Dalrymple
Printed by BAS Printers Ltd